Table Of Contents

Introduction

Why QuickBooks Online is a must-have for small business owners

As a small business owner, you are likely always on the lookout for ways to streamline your business operations and increase efficiency. One tool that can help you achieve these goals is QuickBooks Online. Here are just a few reasons why QuickBooks Online is a must-have for small business owners.

First and foremost, QuickBooks Online can help you stay organized and keep track of your finances. With QuickBooks Online, you can easily create and manage invoices, track expenses, and view financial reports. This can save you time and help you make informed decisions about your business.

QuickBooks Online also offers a range of features that can help you manage your business more effectively. For example, you can use QuickBooks Online to track your inventory, manage your payroll, and even accept online payments from your customers. These features can help you run your business more efficiently and provide a better experience for your customers.

Another advantage of QuickBooks Online is that it is cloud-based, meaning you can access your financial information from anywhere with an internet connection. This is particularly helpful if you have multiple locations or if you need to work remotely. Plus, because QuickBooks Online automatically backs up your data, you can rest assured that your financial information is safe and secure.

Finally, QuickBooks Online is user-friendly and easy to use, even if you have no prior experience with accounting software. There are also a number of resources available to help you get started, including online tutorials and customer support.

In short, if you are a small business owner, QuickBooks Online is a must-have tool that can help you manage your finances, streamline your operations, and grow your business. Whether you are just starting out or looking to take your business to the next level, QuickBooks Online can help you achieve your goals.

What to expect from the course

As a small business owner, you know how important it is to keep your finances in order. QuickBooks Online is a powerful tool that can help you do just that. But if you're new to the software, it can be intimidating. That's where this course comes in. In this chapter, we'll take a look at what you can expect to learn from the Ultimate QuickBooks Online Crash Course for Small Business Owners.

First and foremost, you'll learn how to set up QuickBooks Online for your business. This includes creating your company profile, setting up your chart of accounts, and connecting your bank and credit card accounts. We'll walk you through each step of the process so you can get up and running quickly and easily.

Once your account is set up, we'll dive into the nitty-gritty of using QuickBooks Online. You'll learn how to enter transactions, including sales, expenses, and payments. We'll also cover how to reconcile your accounts and run reports to get a clear picture of your business's financial health.

But QuickBooks Online is more than just a bookkeeping tool. It also offers powerful features like invoicing, inventory management, and payroll. We'll show you how to use these features to streamline your business processes and save time.

Throughout the course, we'll also provide tips and best practices for using QuickBooks Online effectively. You'll learn how to customize your account to fit your specific business needs and how to avoid common mistakes that can cause headaches down the line.

By the end of this course, you'll be a QuickBooks Online pro. You'll have the tools and knowledge you need to keep your finances in order, make informed business decisions, and take your small business to the next level. So let's get started!

How to best use the book

As a small business owner, you already know how important it is to keep track of your finances. QuickBooks Online is a powerful tool that can help you do just that. However, like any tool, it's only as useful as you make it. In this subchapter, we'll explore some tips on how to best use the book to get the most out of your QuickBooks Online experience.

First, it's important to understand the structure of the book. The Ultimate QuickBooks Online Crash Course for Small Business Owners is divided into chapters that cover different aspects of the software, such as setting up your account, managing transactions, and generating reports. Each chapter includes step-by-step instructions and screenshots to help you follow along.

To get the most out of the book, we recommend following along with your own QuickBooks Online account. This will allow you to practice the tasks as you read about them, which will help reinforce your understanding of the material. Don't worry if you make mistakes – that's part of the learning process.

Another tip is to take advantage of the practice exercises and quizzes included in each chapter. These are designed to test your knowledge and help you identify areas where you may need more practice. By completing these exercises, you'll not only reinforce your understanding of the material, but you'll also get a sense of how well you're retaining the information.

If you're feeling overwhelmed by the amount of information in the book, don't worry – you don't have to read it cover to cover. Instead, focus on the chapters that are most relevant to your business. For example, if you primarily use QuickBooks Online for invoicing and payment processing, you may want to focus on the chapters that cover those topics.

Finally, don't be afraid to ask for help. QuickBooks Online has a robust help center and community forum where you can find answers to your questions. You can also reach out to a QuickBooks Online expert or consultant for personalized advice.

By following these tips, you'll be well on your way to mastering QuickBooks Online and taking control of your finances. Remember, the key is to practice, stay engaged, and don't be afraid to ask for help when you need it.

Setting up QuickBooks Online for your Business

Choosing the right QuickBooks Online subscription plan

Choosing the right QuickBooks Online subscription plan is essential for small business owners who want to manage their finances effectively. QuickBooks Online offers a range of subscription plans that cater to different business needs. Each plan comes with unique features and pricing, making it important to choose the best one that fits your business's specific requirements.

The first step in choosing the right QuickBooks Online subscription plan is to evaluate your business needs. Identify the size of your business, the number of employees, and the complexity of your financial transactions. This information will help you determine the plan that best suits your business.

QuickBooks Online offers four main subscription plans: Simple Start, Essentials, Plus, and Advanced. The Simple Start plan is suitable for small businesses with basic accounting needs. It includes features such as tracking income and expenses, creating and sending invoices, and accepting payments online.

The Essentials plan is ideal for small businesses that require more advanced features such as managing bills, time tracking, and multiple users. The Plus plan offers all the features of the Essentials plan plus inventory management and project profitability tracking.

The Advanced plan is designed for larger businesses with more complex accounting needs. It includes features such as custom user permissions, batch invoicing, and advanced reporting. This plan is best suited for businesses with multiple locations or departments.

When choosing a QuickBooks Online subscription plan, it is important to consider the pricing. Each plan comes with a different monthly fee, and the cost increases as you move up to more advanced plans. It is important to choose a plan that fits your budget and offers the features you need to manage your finances effectively.

In conclusion, choosing the right QuickBooks Online subscription plan is crucial for small business owners who want to manage their finances efficiently. Evaluate your business needs, consider the features and pricing of each plan, and choose the one that best fits your requirements and budget. With the right plan, you can streamline your accounting processes, save time, and focus on growing your business.

Setting up your company profile

Setting up your company profile is an essential step in starting and managing your business. It is crucial to have accurate and up-to-date information in your company profile, as it will be used for financial reports, invoices, and other business transactions. In this chapter, we will guide you through the process of setting up your company profile in QuickBooks Online.

First, you need to sign up for a QuickBooks Online account, which you can do by visiting the QuickBooks website. Once you have signed up, you can start creating your company profile. You will need to provide basic information, such as your company name, address, and contact details.

Next, you will need to set up your chart of accounts. This is a list of all the accounts you will use for your business, such as income, expenses, assets, and liabilities. QuickBooks Online has a default chart of accounts, but you can customize it to suit your business needs.

You will also need to set up your products and services. This includes adding items that you sell or services that you provide. You can also add prices and descriptions for each item or service.

Additionally, you will need to set up your payment and bank accounts. This includes adding your bank account details, credit card details, and other payment methods you accept.

One important aspect of setting up your company profile is selecting the correct tax settings. You will need to choose your tax agency and set up your tax rates for sales tax, VAT, and other applicable taxes.

Finally, you can customize your company profile by adding your logo, creating custom invoices and forms, and setting up user access and permissions.

In conclusion, setting up your company profile in QuickBooks Online is an essential step in managing your business finances. By following the steps outlined in this chapter, you can ensure that your company profile is accurate and up-to-date, which will help you stay on top of your finances and make informed business decisions.

Setting up your chart of accounts

Setting up your chart of accounts is an essential step in managing your business finances. The chart of accounts is a list of all the accounts you use in your financial transactions. It helps you categorize and organize all the financial activities of your business, making it easier to track and manage your income and expenses.

In QuickBooks Online, you can easily set up your chart of accounts. The software comes with a standard set of accounts, but you can customize it to fit your business needs. To start, go to the Gear icon and select Chart of Accounts.

The chart of accounts is divided into five categories: Assets, Liabilities, Equity, Income, and Expenses. Assets are what your business owns, such as cash, inventory, and equipment. Liabilities are what your business owes, such as loans and bills. Equity is the value of your business after subtracting liabilities from assets. Income is the money your business earns, and expenses are the money your business spends.

When setting up your chart of accounts, it's essential to create accounts that accurately reflect your business's financial activities. For example, if you are a restaurant owner, you may want to create accounts for food and beverage costs, labor costs, and rent expenses.

You should also consider the level of detail you want in your chart of accounts. Having too many accounts can make it difficult to manage, while too few accounts can make it challenging to track your finances accurately. It's essential to strike a balance between detail and simplicity.

Once you have set up your chart of accounts, it's crucial to maintain it regularly. You should review and update your accounts regularly to ensure they reflect your current financial activities. This will help you stay on top of your finances and make informed business decisions.

In conclusion, setting up your chart of accounts is a crucial step in managing your business finances. Take the time to customize your chart of accounts to fit your business needs and maintain it regularly to ensure it accurately reflects your financial activities. With a well-organized chart of accounts, you'll have the information you need to make informed business decisions and ensure the financial success of your business.

Setting up customers and vendors

Setting up customers and vendors is a crucial step for any small business owner using QuickBooks Online. It is essential to have accurate and up-to-date records of all your customers and vendors to ensure that your business runs smoothly. In this subchapter, we will guide you through the process of setting up customers and vendors in QuickBooks Online.

To begin, you need to create a new customer or vendor account in QuickBooks Online. You can do this by clicking on the "Customers" or "Vendors" tab on the left-hand side of the screen and selecting "New Customer" or "New Vendor". From there, you will be prompted to fill in the necessary details, such as the name, contact information, and billing address.

Once you have created a customer or vendor account, you can start adding transactions. For example, when you issue an invoice to a customer, you can select their name from the drop-down menu in the "Customer" field. This will automatically populate their contact information, making the invoicing process quick and efficient.

Similarly, when you receive a bill from a vendor, you can select their name from the drop-down menu in the "Vendor" field. This will automatically populate their contact information, making it easy to track your expenses and payments to that vendor.

One of the most significant benefits of using QuickBooks Online is that it allows you to track outstanding balances for both customers and vendors. This means that you can easily keep track of who owes you money and who you owe money to, which is essential for maintaining a healthy cash flow.

In addition to setting up customers and vendors, QuickBooks Online also allows you to set up payment terms and methods, create purchase orders, and manage inventory. These features can help you streamline your business operations and improve your overall efficiency.

In conclusion, setting up customers and vendors in QuickBooks Online is a critical step for any small business owner. By keeping accurate and up-to-date records of all your transactions, you can ensure that your business runs smoothly and efficiently. With the help of QuickBooks Online, you can easily manage your customers and vendors, track outstanding balances, and streamline your business operations.

Navigating QuickBooks Online

Understanding the QuickBooks Online dashboard

Understanding the QuickBooks Online dashboard

The QuickBooks Online dashboard is the first thing you see when you log into your QuickBooks Online account. It provides a quick overview of your business's financial performance, including income, expenses, and profits. The dashboard is customizable, so you can choose which widgets to display and where to place them.

The default dashboard includes several widgets, such as the Income Tracker, Expenses, Profit and Loss, and Account Balances. These widgets provide a snapshot of your business's financial health and can be customized to display the data that's most important to you.

The Income Tracker is a powerful tool that allows you to see your business's income in real-time. It displays all your open invoices, estimates, and sales receipts, so you can see which customers owe you money and how much. The Expenses widget shows your business's expenses by category, so you can see where your money is going.

The Profit and Loss widget is a comprehensive report that shows your business's income, expenses, and net profit over a specified period. This report is essential for understanding your business's financial performance and making informed decisions. The Account Balances widget displays your account balances, including bank accounts, credit cards, and loans.

The QuickBooks Online dashboard is customizable, so you can add or remove widgets to create a personalized view of your business's financial performance. You can also move widgets around to create a layout that works best for you.

In addition to the default widgets, QuickBooks Online offers several add-ons that can be added to your dashboard. These add-ons include integrations with other software, such as PayPal and Shopify, and third-party apps that provide additional functionality, such as time tracking and inventory management.

In conclusion, the QuickBooks Online dashboard is an essential tool for small business owners. It provides a comprehensive overview of your business's financial performance and can be customized to display the data that's most important to you. By understanding the QuickBooks Online dashboard, you can make informed decisions that will help your business grow and succeed.

Navigating the QuickBooks Online menu bar

As a small business owner, navigating the QuickBooks Online menu bar can be overwhelming. However, it is essential to understand the menu bar to make the most of QuickBooks Online. The menu bar is located at the top of the screen and consists of different tabs, each containing a drop-down menu. The tabs include Dashboard, Transactions, Sales, Expenses, Reports, Taxes, Accounting, and Workers.

The Dashboard tab provides an overview of your business, including account balances, recent transactions, and reminders. The Transactions tab allows you to manage your business transactions, including creating and categorizing transactions, such as invoices, bills, and expenses. The Sales tab allows you to create and manage sales transactions, including invoices and sales receipts.

The Expenses tab lets you manage your business expenses, including bills, expenses, and checks. The Reports tab provides a variety of reports to help you track your business finances, including profit and loss statements, balance sheets, and cash flow statements. The Taxes tab helps you manage your business taxes, including tracking sales tax and preparing tax forms.

The Accounting tab allows you to manage your business finances, including setting up bank accounts, credit cards, and loans. The Workers tab lets you manage your employees, including setting up payroll, paying employees, and preparing tax forms.

Navigating the QuickBooks Online menu bar can seem daunting, but it is essential to understand each tab's purpose to manage your business finances effectively. Take the time to explore each tab and its drop-down menus, and don't be afraid to reach out to QuickBooks Online support for assistance. With a little practice, you'll be using QuickBooks Online like a pro in no time.

Using the QuickBooks Online search function

Using the QuickBooks Online search function

One of the most powerful features of QuickBooks Online is its search function. With this tool, you can quickly find transactions, customers, vendors, and more. Here's how to use it effectively.

1. Access the search function

To access the search function, simply click on the magnifying glass icon in the upper right-hand corner of your QuickBooks Online dashboard. This will bring up the search bar.

2. Use keywords

To search for a transaction, customer, or vendor, simply type in a keyword related to the item you're looking for. For example, if you're looking for a customer named John Smith, you could type in "John" or "Smith" to find him.

3. Narrow your search

If you're getting too many results, you can narrow your search by using other filters. For example, you can search for transactions within a certain date range, or transactions with a certain dollar amount.

4. Save your search

If you find yourself using the search function frequently for a certain type of transaction or customer, you can save your search for quick access later. Simply click the "Save" button next to the search bar and give your search a name.

5. Use advanced search

For even more powerful searching capabilities, you can use the advanced search function. This will allow you to search for transactions based on multiple criteria, such as date range, customer name, and transaction type.

By using the search function effectively, you can save time and quickly find the information you need in QuickBooks Online. Take some time to explore the different search filters and see how they can work for your business.

Customizing your QuickBooks Online settings

Customizing your QuickBooks Online settings

QuickBooks Online is a powerful accounting software tool that can help small business owners streamline their financial operations. However, in order to get the most out of the software, it's important to customize your QuickBooks Online settings to fit your specific business needs. Here are some tips on how to customize your QuickBooks Online settings:

1. Choose your accounting method: When you first set up your QuickBooks Online account, you'll need to choose whether you want to use the cash or accrual accounting method. This decision will affect how your financial reports are generated, so it's important to choose the method that best fits your business needs.

2. Customize your chart of accounts: Your chart of accounts is a list of all the accounts you use to track your business finances, such as income, expenses, assets, and liabilities. It's important to customize your chart of accounts to fit your specific business needs, so that you can easily track your financial transactions and generate accurate reports.

3. Set up your sales tax: If your business is required to collect sales tax, you'll need to set up your sales tax in QuickBooks Online. You can choose to set up a single sales tax rate or multiple rates, depending on the requirements of your state or local government.

4. Customize your invoice templates: Your invoices are a reflection of your business, so it's important to customize your invoice templates to fit your brand and style. You can add your logo, choose your font and color scheme, and add custom fields to your invoices to make them more personalized.

5. Set up payment reminders: Late payments can be a major headache for small business owners, so it's important to set up payment reminders in QuickBooks Online. You can choose to send reminders automatically or manually, and you can customize the wording of the reminders to fit your business style.

By customizing your QuickBooks Online settings, you can make the software work for you and your business. Take the time to set up your account properly, and you'll be able to streamline your financial operations and generate accurate reports to help you make informed business decisions. With a little bit of customization, QuickBooks Online can be a powerful tool for small business owners.

Entering Transactions in QuickBooks Online

Entering sales receipts

Entering sales receipts is a crucial step in managing your small business finances. This process helps you track and record all the transactions your business makes, which is essential for accurate accounting and tax purposes. QuickBooks Online makes it easy for you to enter sales receipts, and this subchapter will guide you through the process.

First, log in to your QuickBooks Online account and click on the "+" icon in the top right corner of the screen. From the dropdown menu, select "Sales Receipt." This will take you to a new screen where you can start entering the details of your sales receipt.

On the sales receipt form, you'll need to enter the customer's name, the products or services sold, the price, and any applicable discounts or taxes. QuickBooks Online will automatically calculate the total amount due based on this information. If you've already created an invoice for this sale, you can link the sales receipt to the invoice by selecting it from the dropdown menu.

You can also add payment details to the sales receipt, including the payment method, date, and amount. If the payment is not received in full, you can enter a partial payment and update the sales receipt when the remaining balance is paid.

Once you've entered all the necessary information, you can save the sales receipt and print or email it to the customer. QuickBooks Online will automatically update your financial statements and reports based on the information you've entered.

Entering sales receipts regularly is essential for keeping your financial records up-to-date and accurate. It also helps you track your business's cash flow and monitor your sales performance. With QuickBooks Online, you can easily manage your sales receipts and stay on top of your finances.

Entering invoices

Entering Invoices

Entering invoices in QuickBooks Online can be a breeze if you know where to start. Invoices are essential to small business owners as they help you keep track of sales and payments. In this subchapter, we will cover everything you need to know about entering invoices in QuickBooks Online.

Firstly, let's start by defining what an invoice is. An invoice is a document that lists the products or services you provided to a customer, along with the price and any applicable taxes. It also includes payment terms and due dates. You can create and send invoices in QuickBooks Online to your customers, and they can pay you online through various payment methods.

To enter an invoice in QuickBooks Online, follow these steps:

1. Go to the "+New" button on the top left corner of your screen and select "Invoice."

2. Select the customer you want to invoice. If you haven't added the customer yet, click "Add new" to create a new customer profile.

3. Fill in the details of the invoice, including the product or service, the quantity, and the price. If you have multiple products or services, you can add them by clicking "Add another line."

4. Add any applicable taxes or discounts to the invoice.

5. Set the payment terms, due date, and payment method for the invoice.

6. Review the invoice and make any necessary changes.

7. Save and send the invoice to your customer through email or download it as a PDF.

Once the invoice is sent, it will appear in your "Sales" tab in QuickBooks Online. You can track the invoice's status, whether it's paid, overdue, or pending. You can also send reminders to customers who haven't paid their invoices yet.

Entering invoices in QuickBooks Online can save you time and help you keep track of your sales and payments. With these simple steps, you can easily create and send invoices to your customers and stay on top of your business finances.

Entering bills and expenses

Entering bills and expenses is an essential part of managing your small business finances. QuickBooks Online makes it easy to keep track of your bills and expenses, so you always know where your money is going. In this subchapter, we'll walk you through the steps of entering bills and expenses in QuickBooks Online.

First, let's define what bills and expenses are. Bills are amounts owed to vendors or suppliers for goods or services received, but not yet paid for. Expenses, on the other hand, are costs incurred in the operation of your business, such as rent, utilities, and office supplies.

To enter a bill, go to the "Expenses" tab in QuickBooks Online and select "New Expense". From there, select "Bill" and enter the vendor's name, the due date, and the amount due. You can also add a memo to remind yourself what the bill is for. Once you've entered all the necessary information, click "Save and close".

When it's time to pay the bill, go to the "Expenses" tab and select "Pay Bills". Choose the bills you want to pay and the payment method, then click "Save and close". QuickBooks Online will automatically update your accounts payable balance and create a record of the payment.

To enter an expense, go to the "Expenses" tab and select "New Expense". Choose the expense category, enter the amount, and add a memo if necessary. You can also attach a receipt to the expense for record-keeping purposes. Click "Save and close" when you're done.

QuickBooks Online also allows you to set up recurring bills and expenses, which can save you time and ensure that you never miss a payment. To set up a recurring bill or expense, go to the "Expenses" tab and select "New Expense". Choose "Make recurring" and enter the necessary information, such as the frequency and start date. QuickBooks Online will automatically create a new bill or expense for you according to the schedule you set.

Entering bills and expenses in QuickBooks Online is a simple and straightforward process that can help you stay on top of your finances. By keeping accurate records of your bills and expenses, you can make informed decisions about your business and ensure that you're always in control of your cash flow.

Entering payments and deposits

Entering payments and deposits is a crucial aspect of any small business's accounting process. QuickBooks Online offers several tools and features to make this step simpler and more efficient.

To enter a payment or deposit, start by navigating to the "+ New" button on the top left of your QuickBooks Online dashboard. From there, select "Receive Payment" or "Record Deposit" depending on the type of transaction you're entering.

When entering a payment, you'll need to select the customer who made the payment, the payment date, the amount received, and the payment method. You can also add a memo to provide additional information about the transaction.

For deposits, you'll need to select the bank account where the deposit is being made, the deposit date, the amount being deposited, and any additional information about the source of the deposit.

One useful feature in QuickBooks Online is the ability to link payments and deposits to specific invoices or sales receipts. This helps ensure that your records are accurate and up-to-date, and makes it easier to reconcile your accounts.

If you're working with multiple currencies or have international customers, QuickBooks Online also offers tools to help manage foreign currency payments and deposits. You can set up exchange rates and track gains or losses due to currency fluctuations.

It's important to note that entering payments and deposits accurately is crucial for maintaining the financial health of your small business. QuickBooks Online offers several reports and tools to help you stay on top of your finances, including the Profit and Loss report, the Balance Sheet report, and the Statement of Cash Flows. By regularly entering and reviewing your payments and deposits, you can ensure that your financial records are accurate and up-to-date, and make informed decisions about the future of your business.

Managing Accounts Receivable and Accounts Payable

Managing your accounts receivable

Managing your accounts receivable is an essential task for small business owners who want to maintain healthy cash flow and avoid financial problems. Accounts receivable refers to the money that your customers owe you for goods or services you have provided but have not yet been paid for. If you don't manage your accounts receivable effectively, you risk losing track of outstanding payments, which can lead to cash flow problems and even bankruptcy.

To manage your accounts receivable effectively, you need to keep track of all invoices you have sent to customers and when they are due to be paid. You should also have a system in place for following up on overdue payments, such as sending reminder emails or making phone calls. QuickBooks Online is an excellent tool for managing your accounts receivable, as it allows you to create and send invoices, track payments, and set up automatic reminders.

When creating invoices in QuickBooks Online, make sure to include all necessary information, such as the customer's name and address, a description of the goods or services provided, and the payment terms. You can customize your invoices to include your logo and branding, which can help create a professional image for your business. Once you have sent an invoice, you can track its status in QuickBooks Online and see when it has been paid or is overdue.

To follow up on overdue payments, QuickBooks Online allows you to set up automatic reminders that will send emails to customers reminding them to pay their invoices. You can also track customer payment history and see which customers are consistently late in paying their bills. If a customer is repeatedly late in paying, you may need to consider setting up stricter payment terms or even terminating the business relationship.

Managing your accounts receivable can be time-consuming, but it is essential for maintaining a healthy cash flow and avoiding financial problems. QuickBooks Online makes it easy to create invoices, track payments, and follow up on overdue payments, so you can focus on running your business. By staying on top of your accounts receivable, you can ensure that your business stays financially stable and successful.

Managing your accounts payable

Managing your accounts payable is an essential aspect of any small business. Accounts payable refers to the money you owe to your vendors, suppliers, and other creditors. It can include anything from office supplies to rent and utilities.

In QuickBooks Online, managing your accounts payable is easy and straightforward. The first thing you need to do is set up your vendors. This includes entering their contact information, payment terms, and any other relevant details. You can also set up recurring bills if you have regular expenses that you pay every month.

Once your vendors are set up, you can start entering bills into QuickBooks Online. This includes the amount you owe, the due date, and any other relevant details. You can also attach any supporting documents, such as invoices or receipts.

When it comes time to pay your bills, you can either pay them manually or set up automatic payments. QuickBooks Online makes it easy to pay bills with just a few clicks. You can also schedule payments in advance to ensure that your bills are always paid on time.

One of the benefits of using QuickBooks Online to manage your accounts payable is that it allows you to track your expenses in real-time. You can see how much you owe to each vendor, which bills are due soon, and how much you have spent on different expense categories.

Another important aspect of managing your accounts payable is keeping track of your cash flow. QuickBooks Online allows you to see your cash flow in real-time, so you can make informed decisions about when to pay your bills and how much to pay.

In conclusion, managing your accounts payable is an essential part of running a small business. QuickBooks Online makes it easy to keep track of your bills, pay them on time, and manage your cash flow. By staying on top of your accounts payable, you can ensure that your business runs smoothly and efficiently.

Running reports to track your accounts receivable and accounts payable

Running reports to track your accounts receivable and accounts payable is a critical aspect of managing your small business's finances. QuickBooks Online offers a wide range of reports that can help you keep track of your accounts receivable and accounts payable, allowing you to make informed decisions and take necessary actions to ensure your business stays healthy.

To run a report on your accounts receivable, go to the Reports tab in QuickBooks Online and click on Customers & Receivables. From there, you can choose from a variety of reports, such as the Invoice List, the Accounts Receivable Aging Summary, and the Open Invoices report. These reports will provide you with detailed information about the invoices you have sent out to customers, including the invoice date, due date, and amount owed. You can use this information to follow up with customers who have outstanding balances and ensure that you receive payment in a timely manner.

To run a report on your accounts payable, go to the Reports tab in QuickBooks Online and click on Vendors & Payables. From there, you can choose from a variety of reports, such as the Unpaid Bills report, the Accounts Payable Aging Summary, and the Vendor Balance Detail report. These reports will provide you with detailed information about the bills you owe to vendors, including the bill date, due date, and amount owed. You can use this information to ensure that you pay your bills on time and avoid late fees and interest charges.

By regularly running reports on your accounts receivable and accounts payable, you can stay on top of your business's finances and make informed decisions about cash flow, budgeting, and other financial matters. QuickBooks Online makes it easy to generate these reports and keep track of your financial data, allowing you to focus on running and growing your business. With the right tools and knowledge, you can take control of your finances and achieve success as a small business owner.

Reconciling Bank and Credit Card Accounts

Understanding bank and credit card reconciliation

Understanding bank and credit card reconciliation is an essential aspect of bookkeeping for small business owners. It is the process of comparing and matching the transactions recorded in your QuickBooks Online account with those on your bank or credit card statements to ensure that they are accurate and complete. This process helps you to identify any discrepancies, errors, or fraudulent transactions that may occur in your business accounts.

Reconciliation is necessary because it helps you to keep track of your cash flow and ensure that your financial records are up-to-date. It also helps you to avoid overdrafts, bounced checks, and other financial problems that could negatively impact your business.

To reconcile your bank and credit card accounts in QuickBooks Online, you need to follow the following steps:

1. Log in to your QuickBooks Online account and select the "Accounting" tab.

2. Click on the "Reconcile" option under the "Tools" menu.

3. Select the account you want to reconcile from the drop-down menu.

4. Enter the statement date and ending balance from your bank or credit card statement.

5. Check the transactions that match those on your statement and adjust any discrepancies or errors.

6. Click on the "Finish Now" button to complete the reconciliation process.

It is essential to reconcile your bank and credit card accounts regularly, ideally every month, to ensure that your financial records are accurate and up-to-date. This process helps you to catch any errors or fraudulent transactions early and take appropriate action to protect your business.

In summary, understanding bank and credit card reconciliation is crucial for small business owners to ensure that their financial records are accurate and up-to-date. By reconciling your accounts regularly, you can identify any discrepancies, errors, or fraudulent transactions and take appropriate action to protect your business.

Reconciling your bank accounts in QuickBooks Online

Reconciling your bank accounts in QuickBooks Online is an important task that small business owners should carry out regularly. It involves ensuring that the transactions in your QuickBooks Online account match those in your bank account. This process is essential because it helps you identify any discrepancies that may arise, such as errors or fraudulent transactions.

To reconcile your bank accounts in QuickBooks Online, you need to follow a few simple steps. First, you need to gather your bank statements and compare the transactions listed with those in your QuickBooks account. You can do this by clicking on the "Reconcile" button on your QuickBooks dashboard and selecting the bank account you want to reconcile.

Next, you need to enter the ending balance from your bank statement and compare it with the balance in your QuickBooks account. If the two balances match, you can proceed with the reconciliation process. However, if there are any discrepancies, you need to identify the cause and make the necessary adjustments.

When reconciling your bank accounts in QuickBooks Online, it's essential to ensure that all transactions are properly recorded. This means that you need to categorize expenses and income correctly and ensure that all transactions are entered in a timely manner. This will help you avoid errors and ensure that your financial reports are accurate.

In conclusion, reconciling your bank accounts in QuickBooks Online is an essential task that small business owners should carry out regularly. It helps you identify any discrepancies that may arise and ensures that your financial reports are accurate. By following the simple steps outlined above, you can reconcile your bank accounts in QuickBooks Online with ease and confidence.

Reconciling your credit card accounts in QuickBooks Online

Reconciling your credit card accounts in QuickBooks Online

If you have a small business, you probably use a credit card to cover your expenses. It's essential to keep track of your credit card transactions and reconcile them regularly to avoid errors and confusion. QuickBooks Online makes it easy to reconcile your credit card accounts, ensuring that your financial records are accurate and up-to-date.

To reconcile your credit card accounts in QuickBooks Online, follow these steps:

Step 1: Open the Reconcile page
From the Dashboard, click on the Gear icon and select Reconcile. Choose the credit card account that you want to reconcile.

Step 2: Enter statement information
Enter your credit card statement's ending date and balance. QuickBooks Online will compare this information to your transactions to ensure that everything matches.

Step 3: Review transactions

QuickBooks Online will display all transactions for the selected period. Review each transaction to ensure that it matches your credit card statement. Check for any discrepancies, such as duplicate transactions or missing payments.

Step 4: Mark transactions as cleared

Once you have reviewed all transactions, mark them as cleared. Click on the checkbox next to each transaction to mark it as cleared. This indicates that you have verified that the transaction matches your credit card statement.

Step 5: Finish reconciling

If everything matches, click on the Finish now button to complete the reconciliation process. QuickBooks Online will update your accounts and mark the reconciliation as complete.

Reconciling your credit card accounts in QuickBooks Online is crucial to maintaining accurate financial records. It can help you identify errors and discrepancies, preventing potential issues down the line. By following these simple steps, you can ensure that your credit card accounts are reconciled correctly and up-to-date.

In conclusion, reconciling your credit card accounts in QuickBooks Online is an essential task for small business owners. It helps ensure that your financial records are accurate and up-to-date, providing you with a clear picture of your business's financial health. By following the steps outlined above, you can easily reconcile your credit card accounts and avoid any potential errors or discrepancies.

Reporting and Analyzing Your Business in QuickBooks Online

Running financial reports

Running financial reports is an essential task for any small business owner using QuickBooks Online. It provides a detailed picture of the financial health of your business and helps you make informed decisions about its future.

To run financial reports in QuickBooks Online, follow these simple steps:

Step 1: Navigate to the Reports tab on the left-hand side menu.

Step 2: Choose the type of report you want to run from the list of categories. For example, you might want to run a profit and loss report, a balance sheet, or a cash flow statement.

Step 3: Customize the report to suit your needs by selecting the date range, choosing which accounts to include, and selecting other filters if necessary.

Step 4: Run the report and review the results. You can export the report to Excel or PDF if you need to share it with others.

Running financial reports regularly can help you track your business's progress and identify areas for improvement. For example, you might notice that your expenses are higher than your revenue, indicating that you need to cut costs or increase sales. Or you might see that your cash flow is tight, suggesting that you need to focus on collecting payments from customers more quickly.

By running financial reports in QuickBooks Online, you can take control of your business's finances and make informed decisions that will help you succeed. Whether you're just starting out or have been in business for years, taking the time to run financial reports can help you stay on top of your finances and achieve your goals.

Analyzing your business with QuickBooks Online

As a small business owner, it is important to keep track of the financial health of your business. One of the best ways to do this is to use QuickBooks Online, a cloud-based accounting software that helps you manage your finances, track expenses, and generate reports.

Analyzing your business with QuickBooks Online can provide you with valuable insights into your business. You can use QuickBooks Online to analyze your profit and loss, cash flow, and balance sheet. By analyzing these reports, you can identify areas where you can cut costs, increase revenue, and improve your overall financial performance.

To get started with analyzing your business with QuickBooks Online, you will need to set up your account and connect your bank and credit card accounts. Once you have done this, you can start tracking your income and expenses.

One of the most valuable features of QuickBooks Online is its reporting capabilities. You can generate reports on a wide range of financial metrics, including revenue, expenses, profit and loss, cash flow, and more. These reports can help you identify trends and patterns in your business, and help you make decisions about where to focus your efforts.

Another helpful feature of QuickBooks Online is its integration with other business tools, such as payroll services, time tracking software, and invoicing tools. By integrating these tools with QuickBooks Online, you can streamline your business operations and make it easier to manage your finances.

In conclusion, analyzing your business with QuickBooks Online is essential for small business owners who want to stay on top of their finances and improve their overall financial performance. By using QuickBooks Online to track your income and expenses, generate reports, and integrate with other business tools, you can gain valuable insights into your business and make informed decisions about where to focus your efforts.

Customizing and saving reports in QuickBooks Online

Customizing and saving reports in QuickBooks Online

As a small business owner, keeping track of your finances is crucial to the success of your business. QuickBooks Online provides a variety of reports that help you understand your financial situation and make informed decisions. However, sometimes the default reports may not provide the information you need, or you may want to customize the report to suit your specific needs.

Customizing reports in QuickBooks Online is easy and allows you to tailor reports to your business needs. You can modify the columns, filters, and headers to display the information that is most important to you. Here's how to customize a report in QuickBooks Online:

1. Go to the Reports tab and select the report you want to customize.

2. Click on the Customize button located at the top-right corner of the report.

3. Use the customization panel on the left-hand side to modify the report. You can add or remove columns, change the date range, apply filters, and more.

4. As you make changes, the report will update in real-time, so you can see how the changes affect the report.

5. Once you are satisfied with the changes, click on the Run report button to save the customized report.

Saving customized reports in QuickBooks Online

Once you have customized a report, you can save it for future use. This saves you time and effort in recreating the report each time you need it. Here's how to save a customized report in QuickBooks Online:

1. After customizing the report, click on the Save customization button located at the top-right corner of the report.

2. Give the report a name and select the folder where you want to save it.

3. Click on the Save button to save the report.

4. To access the saved report, go to the Reports tab and select the Saved reports tab. Here you will find all the reports you have saved.

In conclusion, customizing and saving reports in QuickBooks Online is a great way to get the information you need to make informed decisions. By following the steps outlined above, you can easily customize and save reports that suit your specific needs. This feature makes QuickBooks Online a valuable tool for small business owners who want to stay on top of their finances.

Integrating QuickBooks Online with Third-Party Apps

Understanding QuickBooks Online integrations

Understanding QuickBooks Online Integrations

In today's fast-paced business environment, time is of the essence. Small business owners need to work smarter, not harder, to stay ahead of the competition. One way to achieve this is by integrating QuickBooks Online with other applications and tools. QuickBooks Online integrations allow you to streamline your business operations, automate tasks, and save time.

What are QuickBooks Online Integrations?

QuickBooks Online integrations are connections between QuickBooks Online and other software applications or tools. These integrations allow you to transfer data seamlessly between different applications, eliminating the need for manual data entry. There are many QuickBooks Online integrations available, ranging from payment processors to project management tools.

Why should Small Business Owners use QuickBooks Online Integrations?

Small business owners should use QuickBooks Online integrations because they help to simplify and automate their workflow. Integrations reduce the need for manual data entry, which saves time and prevents errors. Furthermore, integrations can help small business owners to manage their finances more effectively by providing real-time data and insights.

What are some of the most popular QuickBooks Online Integrations?

There are many QuickBooks Online integrations available, but some of the most popular ones include:

1. PayPal: PayPal is a payment processor that allows you to accept payments online. With the QuickBooks Online integration, you can automatically record PayPal transactions in QuickBooks Online.

2. Shopify: Shopify is an e-commerce platform that allows you to sell products online. With the QuickBooks Online integration, you can automatically transfer sales data from Shopify to QuickBooks Online.

3. TSheets: TSheets is a time tracking and scheduling tool. With the QuickBooks Online integration, you can automatically transfer time data from TSheets to QuickBooks Online.

4. Expensify: Expensify is an expense tracking tool. With the QuickBooks Online integration, you can automatically transfer expense data from Expensify to QuickBooks Online.

5. Salesforce: Salesforce is a customer relationship management tool. With the QuickBooks Online integration, you can automatically transfer customer data from Salesforce to QuickBooks Online.

In conclusion, QuickBooks Online integrations are essential for small business owners who want to streamline their workflow, automate tasks, and save time. There are many integrations available, and you should choose the ones that best suit your business needs. By using QuickBooks Online integrations, you can take your business to the next level.

Integrating QuickBooks Online with payment processors

Integrating QuickBooks Online with payment processors

One of the most significant hurdles that small business owners face today is managing payments efficiently. Invoicing and receiving payments from customers can be a challenging task, especially if you don't have a streamlined system in place. With QuickBooks Online, the process has become much easier, and you can integrate payment processors like PayPal, Stripe, and Square to make payments more accessible and more efficient for your business.

When you integrate QuickBooks Online with payment processors, you can receive payments directly into your bank account, and the transaction is automatically recorded in QuickBooks. This process eliminates the need for manual data entry, reduces errors, and saves you time.

To integrate payment processors with QuickBooks Online, you need to follow these simple steps:

1. Go to the QuickBooks Online dashboard and click on the gear icon in the top right corner.

2. Select "account and settings" from the drop-down menu.

3. Click on the "payments" tab and select "connect" under the payment processor you want to integrate.

4. Follow the instructions to complete the integration process.

Once the integration is complete, you can start accepting payments directly from your customers through QuickBooks Online. Your customers can pay using their credit or debit cards or even PayPal. The payment is automatically recorded in QuickBooks, and you can easily track the payment status in the system.

Integrating payment processors with QuickBooks Online also provides you with additional benefits like easy invoicing and payment reminders. You can create and send invoices directly from QuickBooks, and your customers can pay the invoice with just a few clicks. You can also set up automatic payment reminders for overdue invoices, which saves you time and helps you get paid faster.

In summary, integrating payment processors with QuickBooks Online is a game-changer for small business owners. It simplifies the payment process, reduces errors, saves time, and provides you with additional benefits like easy invoicing and payment reminders. If you haven't already integrated payment processors with QuickBooks Online, it's time to do so and take your business to the next level.

Integrating QuickBooks Online with other business apps

Integrating QuickBooks Online with other business apps is a powerful way to streamline your business operations, save time, and improve accuracy. QuickBooks Online is already a powerful tool on its own, but when you integrate it with other business apps, it becomes even more valuable. In this chapter, we'll explore some of the benefits of integrating QuickBooks Online with other business apps, and some of the most popular integrations available.

Benefits of Integrating QuickBooks Online with Other Business Apps

Integrating QuickBooks Online with other business apps can provide many benefits to small business owners. Here are just a few:

- Streamlined Data Entry: Integrating QuickBooks Online with other business apps can save you time by reducing the need for double entry. When you enter data into one app, it can automatically sync with QuickBooks Online, so you don't have to enter it again.
- Improved Accuracy: When you're manually entering data into multiple apps, there's a higher risk of errors. Integrating QuickBooks Online with other business apps can reduce this risk by syncing the data automatically.
- Better Reporting: When you integrate QuickBooks Online with other business apps, you can get better insights into your business. You can pull data from multiple sources and create custom reports that show you exactly what you need to know.
- More Efficient Workflows: By integrating QuickBooks Online with other business apps, you can create more efficient workflows. For example, you can set up automatic reminders for unpaid invoices or create automatic purchase orders when inventory levels get low.

Popular QuickBooks Online Integrations

There are many different apps that integrate with QuickBooks Online. Here are a few of the most popular:

- PayPal: You can automatically import PayPal transactions into QuickBooks Online and reconcile them with your bank account.
- TSheets: This app allows you to track employee time and sync it with QuickBooks Online for accurate payroll processing.
- Shopify: If you have an online store, you can integrate it with QuickBooks Online to automatically sync sales data and inventory levels.
- Expensify: This app makes expense tracking easy by allowing you to scan receipts with your phone and import them into QuickBooks Online.

Integrating QuickBooks Online with other business apps can provide many benefits to small business owners. By streamlining data entry, improving accuracy, providing better reporting, and creating more efficient workflows, you can save time and run your business more effectively. With so many integrations available, it's easy to find the right combination of apps to suit your needs.

Conclusion

Review of key takeaways

Review of Key Takeaways

Congratulations! You've completed "The Ultimate QuickBooks Online Crash Course for Small Business Owners." By now, you have learned many important tips and tricks for managing your small business finances with QuickBooks Online. Here is a review of the key takeaways from this course.

1. Choose the Right Plan

QuickBooks Online offers various plans that cater to different business needs. It is important to choose the plan that best suits your business requirements. Take the time to evaluate your needs and budget before deciding on a plan.

2. Set Up Your Company File Correctly

The company file is the heart of your QuickBooks Online account. It is important to set it up correctly, including your company information, chart of accounts, and preferences. This will ensure that you can manage your finances efficiently and effectively.

3. Customize Your Invoices and Sales Forms

Your invoices and sales forms are important documents that represent your business. Customize them to reflect your brand image and include all the necessary information. This will help you get paid on time and make a good impression on your customers.

4. Manage Your Expenses

Tracking your expenses is crucial for understanding your business's financial health. Use QuickBooks Online to record all your expenses, including bills, receipts, and credit card transactions. This will help you stay on top of your cash flow and make informed financial decisions.

5. Reconcile Your Bank Accounts Regularly

Reconciling your bank accounts is an essential part of managing your finances. It helps you identify any discrepancies between your records and your bank statements. This will help you catch any errors or fraud early and keep your accounts accurate.

6. Generate Reports

QuickBooks Online offers various reports that can help you understand your business's financial performance. Use these reports to analyze your income, expenses, and profits. This will help you make informed decisions and plan for the future.

In conclusion, QuickBooks Online is a powerful tool for managing your small business finances. By following the tips and tricks outlined in this course, you can use QuickBooks Online to its fullest potential and take your business to the next level. Good luck!

Next steps for mastering QuickBooks Online

Now that you have a good grasp of the basics of QuickBooks Online, it's time to take your skills to the next level. Here are some next steps for mastering QuickBooks Online:

1. Customize Your Chart of Accounts: The chart of accounts is the backbone of your accounting system. It categorizes all your transactions and helps you generate financial reports. Customizing it to fit your business needs can help you get more accurate information.

2. Set Up Users and Permissions: If you have employees or an accountant who need to access your QuickBooks account, you can set up users and give them different levels of access. This way, you can control who can view or edit certain information.

3. Use the Bank Feeds Feature: QuickBooks Online's bank feeds feature allows you to connect your bank accounts and credit cards to your QuickBooks account. This makes it easy to reconcile your accounts and track your expenses.

4. Explore Third-Party Apps: QuickBooks Online integrates with hundreds of third-party apps that can help you streamline your business processes. From inventory management to time tracking, there's an app for almost everything.

5. Get Certified: If you want to take your QuickBooks skills to the next level, you can become a QuickBooks Certified User. This certification program is designed to teach you advanced skills and best practices for using QuickBooks Online.

6. Attend Training and Workshops: QuickBooks Online offers a range of training and workshops, both online and in-person. These can be a great way to learn new skills and network with other small business owners.

By taking these next steps, you can become a QuickBooks Online expert and get the most out of your accounting system. With accurate financial information at your fingertips, you can make informed decisions that will help your business thrive.

Additional resources for small business owners.

As a small business owner, it's important to have access to additional resources to help you grow and manage your business effectively. Here are a few resources you can use to supplement your QuickBooks Online knowledge and expand your skillset.

1. QuickBooks Community - The QuickBooks Community is a great place to connect with other small business owners and get answers to your QuickBooks questions. You can search for answers to common questions, participate in discussions, and get advice from experts.

2. QuickBooks Online Blog - The QuickBooks Online Blog is a great resource for small business owners looking for tips, tricks, and best practices for using QuickBooks Online. You can find articles on everything from managing your finances to growing your business.

3. Small Business Administration (SBA) - The SBA offers a wide range of resources for small business owners, including access to funding, business counseling, and training programs. They also offer free online courses on topics like marketing, finance, and management.

4. SCORE - SCORE is a nonprofit organization that provides free business mentoring and education. They offer workshops, webinars, and online courses on a variety of topics, including QuickBooks Online.

5. YouTube - YouTube is a great resource for small business owners looking for tutorials and how-to videos on using QuickBooks Online. There are a number of channels dedicated to QuickBooks Online training, including the official QuickBooks channel.

6. LinkedIn Learning - LinkedIn Learning offers a wide range of online courses on business and technology topics, including QuickBooks Online. You can access their courses for a monthly fee or sign up for a free trial.

By taking advantage of these additional resources, you can expand your knowledge and skills as a small business owner and get the most out of QuickBooks Online. Whether you're looking for advice from experts, training courses, or community support, there's something out there for everyone.

www.ingramcontent.com/pod-product-compliance
Lightning Source LLC
Chambersburg PA
CBHW082150230526

45467CB00043B/2763